Quicksand Secrets

by Howard Johnston

PublishAmerica

Baltimore

First printing

ISBN: 1-4137-2340-3
PUBLISHED BY PUBLISHAMERICA, LLLP
www.publishamerica.com
Baltimore

Printed in the United States of America

Acknowledgment

In addition to recognizing the support of my parents, I would like to acknowledge a few influential people in my life:

Hilda Matero, my librarian grandmother, for introducing me to the world of literature;

Sherman Alexie for crafting beautiful poems of living in hopeless situations;

Charles Bukowski for openly and honestly writing about his demons, his mistakes, his ignorance;

Johnny Cash for singing about sinners and outlaws seeking redemption, or at least peace of mind.

Robert Fisher, my high school writing teacher, for encouraging me to never let the world sand down my rough edges.

My wife and son, for always being there to pull me from the quicksand.

1.

Death, Loss and the Overanalyzing Machine

Autumn, the Season of Dying

"we are living too short
and dying too long"

Spring is birth, summer life,
Autumn, the season of dying,
Winter, the frozen sleep of death.

Autumn is the prelude
  gradual or abrupt
To winter's eternal slumber
When vibrant leaves turn gold
  then brown
    then wither away
Dropping to the frostbitten earth
To be raked into piles
  for disposal
Or trapped
Under several feet of snow
Waiting for spring's resurrection.

Autumn is the time
For mothers to gently
Shatter entire families
By leaving
With the bitter crisp wind.
  Pillows don't cushion
  A sledge hammer's blow.

Autumn was the time
She led us upstairs
To the separate bed
  room
To break the news
  and our spirit.

"Little boys need their father."
  We need our mother, too.
"So I will be leaving."
  So will my trust, Mom.

Autumn is the season
For young boys' hearts
To die
  fall to the ground
    and rot under ice and snow.

Autumn, the season of despair
Watching your mother
Turn brittle
As she slowly
  yet bravely
Approaches winter's grasp.

Autumn brings harvest, foliage
Romantic terms
For dying.
Leaves, loved ones, innocence, trust.
It's all birth, life, dying, death.
It's all perpetual death.

Pulse of Life

So often
I mistake the daily
Throbbing, bustling, scurrying,
Maddening grind
For the simple and pure
Pulse of life.

Ulcer breeding
Nose to the grindstone
Heart pumping like a piston
Workaholic haste
Is no substitute
For an ocean breeze
Or the burnt red clouds
Of a Malibu sunset.

I must constantly
Remind myself
To pause for thought
Listen
  truly listen
To jazz classics
And to my son's
Laughter.

Days
No, weeks pass
Before I allow myself
A relaxed, contented smile
Or the time
To savor a precious moment
To read or write a poem.

I pride myself
In self-sacrifice
For the sake of food
On the table.
Yet I deprive myself
Of time spent at peace
Food for the soul
Quiet time
  play time
    my time

Is this the example
I want to set for
My son:
Deny yourself
For the benefit
Of those you love
Rather than enjoy
Life with them.

Goodbye

It is a dark
And cold
New Hampshire night.
The stars observe
And discuss
What they see.
The wind bites
Our cheeks
And nostrils
With its miniature
Razor-sharp teeth.

We walk to a tree
Wondering
If we are facing
The right direction,
If we are doing this
According to tradition.
We whisper
Inner prayers
And last
Good-byes
To the departed.

The tobacco
Is compressed
And damp from sweat
After being held
In the palm
Of my fist
During the entire
Catholic /
Mic Mac
Funeral service,

After being squeezed
Even tighter
While I mumbled my
Eulogy,
Unable to speak up
For fear that
My voice would crack
And the words tumble
Back down my throat,
Unable to look up
From the page
For fear of the
First tear
Which would lead to
A million more,

After resting
At the bottom
Of my pocket,
Waiting for this moment,
To be released
Into the wind
Which the shaman told us
Was the voices of
Ancestors gathering
To whisper
Their goodbyes.

You Laugh

We are exact opposites
And I love you for it.

You laugh
Just to hear
The sound of it.
You make friends
As easily as
Most people make toast.
You can talk
For hours,
Changing subjects,
Shifting gears,
Jumping back to
The point at hand
With unknowing ease.

You don't know
The meaning
Of the word "no."
You have a mind
And a mouth
Of your own.
You have a maddening habit
Of refusing to listen
To any advice
And a knack
For sticking out
In crowds.

You giggle
In the most
Stifled situations.
You ask the most

Unspeakable questions.
You find it
Impossible
To lie
Even when calling in sick.

You are neurotic
About housework.
Cleanliness is beyond
Godliness.
You insist on
An organic diet
For our son.
You won't step foot
Out of the house
Without makeup.

You have telepathic
Sensitivities
For those you hold dear.
You seem to be cursed
With a fragile
Physical frame,
Yet are capable
Of superhuman acts
Of emotional strength.
You continue to amaze me
With your devotion.

We are exact opposites
And I love you for it.

deeper

this week
I got another taste
of the bile
life forces
down your throat.

this week
I was reminded
how fragile our
security is.
you struggle
paycheck
to paycheck,
barely able to pay the rent,
school, car insurance,
health insurance,
groceries, gasoline,
etc., etc., etc...
then life dumps a shit storm
on your head,
pushes you deeper
into debt,
deeper
in the hole,
deeper
into depression.

the car dies,
and imports are
expensive to fix,
even those that are
eight years old.

the dog
gets sick,

or worse,
has to be put
down.

a loved one
passes away,
and you have to
borrow money
for airline tickets
to a funeral
and miss work
in the process.

your wife
gets in a
car accident
that lays her up
for weeks
with no pay,
but a steady
stream of bills

so you try
to crawl out of
this hole,
this debt,
this depression.

but just as
you start
to see light
even a false
hope,
it all starts again.

it's never
just one
thing.

no,
you could
overcome
that.

that would be too
easy.

so you get hit
with three
or four
good shots to the gut.
you sit wondering
is life
really this shitty?
does it ever get
better?
what's the fucking
point?

but you're in
too deep
to quit
now.
others depend on you
financially
emotionally.
others are counting
on you.
"life is hard"
they said
and I didn't
believe them.

now I see
what they meant.

now I see.

Blanket Song

My son and I
Strode into the circle
To pay honor to the
Host Southern Drum
At the 12th annual UCLA
Pow wow,
Dropping money on a blanket
Out of respect
For the songs
And appreciation for the
Miles traveled.

Later that afternoon
Several other blankets
Were laid out
For various worthy causes.
I couldn't help but compare
This scene to the Catholic
Mass we sat through
Where two collections
Were taken
One for the church
Another for the school.
It annoyed me as would
A panhandler
On the same corner
With the identical story
Every single day
Or a musician
On Venice Beach
Playing the same song
Over and over
With guitar case open
For contributions

My cynical mind
Wandered
To past pow wows
And the disheartening truth
Behind the serenity,
Native American children
Vandalizing a building
At Loyola Merrimount
Even after repeated
Announcements for
Parents to control
Their children,
To actually watch
Their kids,
Not to let them run wild.

A pow wow in a tiny
Gymnasium
Where my son
Won a raffle
Yet was not offered
The same prizes as
Darker skinned winners.
They had no way of knowing
He is 1/8 Mic Mac,
Which shouldn't have
Mattered anyway.

Or even the day before
When a majority
Of the gazebo
Dwelling Indians
Full of self-pride
In their jingle dresses
And painted faces
Declined to stand for
Honor songs
When requested to do so.

Especially the teenager
Who adamantly refused
When an elder walked
The circle
Urging the sitters
To be standers
Even if not in their hearts.
She would rather listen
To her Walkman
Than honor a professor
At this university,
A member of the group
Hosting this pow wow,
Who had recently
Passed away.

It is hard
To look past these
Obstacles
To the tradition
And spirit of pow wows,
The dancing tiny tots,
The Aztec friendship dance,
The intertribals,
The ceremonies conducted
For a single fallen
Eagle feather.

As my mind twisted
In sorrowful recognition
Another blanket song
Was announced:
A family traveling
To or from
Another pow wow
A thousand miles away
Was in a tragic car crash
And lost their youngest son.

"This is our way of
Honoring this boy.
This is a pow wow family.
One day you will need help
And others will help you,
But today this family
Needs your help.
This boy will see
You today
And ask the Creator
To bless you."

As the drums steadily beat
And the gourd rattles
Were shaken,
People walked to the blanket
More people than any
Intertribal had seduced
Into the circle,
More people than
I could count,
In fact it seemed as if
More people were coming
To help this family
Than were actually in
Attendance that day,
As if people materialized
Out of thin air
To enter the circle
And come to the aid
Of a family in need.

Three time zones and
Countless heartaches away
A family sees their departed
Sister across the
Pow wow circle
Only for her to disappear
As they run to her.

Can you smell
The sweet smoke
Of burning sage
Sifting and drifting
As it sweeps the soul
And cleanses the heart
As if ancestors
Were fanning a smudge
Stick with sacred feathers.

Just when my cynicism
Grows to its fullest
I am always given
A sign of hope.

I walk silently eastward
As familiar faces
Flicker across the white
Canvas of barren snow,
Peeling birch trees
And empty gray sky.
The cold air bites
At any exposed flesh,
My heart beat slows,
My breath deepens,
My mind relaxes,
My soul smiles
A satisfied smile.

Saco River

Stillness of water trapped
By artificial landscapes
In this urban video game reality
Brings me back in time.

Peace of watching the Saco
Drift through Carroll County,
Languidly caressing riverbanks,
Licking rocks, delivering fish.

The silent rush of river water
Calmly work, work, working its way
Rather than throwing pulsing waves
Onto beleaguered beaches.

For years its smooth current
Brought me sedative solitude
Regardless of the location
I chose to observe its patience.

Skipping stones across its back,
Swinging from a thick knotted rope
Timing my descent for the deepest
Section of the swimming hole.

Clumsily jumping slippery rocks,
Fishing for trout with my father,
Watching autumn's golden foliage
Swept away in the dark brown water,

Standing on the same rocks protruding
Through winter's white blanket,
Water trickling through the partly
Frozen hypothermic trap,

Spring thaws exact nature's revenge,
Flooded river beds empty
Into corn fields, wash out bridges,
Spreading futility like melted butter,

Overlooked undertows
Could drown a horse
While the surface remains
Smooth as glass.

A breeze warms my skin, yet
Ripples shimmer across the Saco
In liquid goose bump patterns.
I let out a sigh of release.

Swimming lessons
  Skinny dipping
    Frozen beach
      Open grave

Today I live in a mega-city
Metropolitan melting pot
With concrete consciousness
Keeping our collective hackles up.

No grass or trees except
Where designs call for insertion
In place of a sidewalk or parking lot.

The sky is blurred by smog
The mountains a far-off promise
Never to be realized.

Even our closest natural wonder
The Pacific ocean
Is a turbulent reminder
Of our turbulent times.

Waves crashing onto shore
Polluted bays are
Unsafe for swimming
Not to mention drinking.

The deadly peace of the Saco
Draws me closer
Come watch men fish for
Tin roofing and red black embers
After someone burned down
The Redstone covered bridge.
Two pieces of land
Divided by the Saco once again.

The deadly peace of the Saco
Draws me closer
Come park your car
On a frozen
New England nightmare
Failed attempt at
Self asphyxiation
Longing to sleep forever
Beside the Saco's tranquility.

City of Angels

From the 28th floor
I view the sprawling
Urban food chain
City streets define
And divide
City blocks
Neighborhoods and
Gated communities

Palm trees veil
Fractured families
Blackened, puffy eyes
Which speak of misery
Loving company

Dusk brings the arrival
Of a fresh set
Of drive-by shootings
Trauma room victims
And date rapes

Streetlights frame
The not-so-obvious
Borders
Darkened alleys harbor
Sadness and secrets
Anonymous
Shouts and screams
Announcing the anger
And anguish
Without an anchor

Manicured lawns
Disguise the discontent
Boarded-up liquor stores
And dead-end derelicts
Declare this corner
No man's land

Paradise burns
Night after night
Yet we awaken to the
Seabreeze sunshine
And the satisfaction of survival
Our candy-coated madness

Bird's eye view
Of a city
Out of control
Beyond control
Disjointed, disconnected
The inhumanity has infected
The inhabitants

The shame twists
Us all into
Emotional pretzels
Doctors driving Beamers
Past winos
Wandering busy boulevards
In bloody, blistered feet

If God is watching
He must be weeping

In Your Shoes

If I were
In your shoes
My heart would
Pound
Day and night
In anticipation

If I were
In your shoes
I'd be scared
To death
By the thought
Of death
Approaching

If I were
In your shoes
I would live
In dread
Knowing a beast
Was preying
On me
Awaiting its time to kill

If I were
In your shoes
I'd lie awake at night
For fear
Of being taken
In my sleep

If I were
In your shoes
I would curse the day

My doctor uttered
Cancer
And released this blood
Thirsty savage
On my trail

If I were
In your shoes
I would sit
With my back to a corner
Talking to myself
Spitting at strangers
Fighting off the madness

If I were
In your shoes
I'd most definitely
View my disease
As an animal
Tracking me down
Toying with me
Choosing the time
To snap my soul
In two

If I were
In your shoes
I'd lose my mind

Mistakes

God, I still hate
Making mistakes
The initial wave of disgust
And the nagging reminder
Of what an incompetent fool
I am

I'm still wrestling
With my demons
The slightest mistake
Tears apart my insides
Stomach acids flow
My intestines twist
Like a filthy sponge
Being wrung out
I pound my head
Against the wall
Repeatedly

I turn around
And stare into my past
Searching for a mistake
To strangle myself with
Poke in the eye
With a sharp stick
Finger down the throat
Voluntary ulcer
Slow motion suicide

I still haven't mastered
The art of letting go
Of my countless mistakes
Forgive and forget
Doesn't apply to self-loathing

I wince at the flashback
And mentally nail myself
To a flaming cross

The worst mistakes
Are the ones sitting in front of me
Constant reminder
Of my stupidity
I can forget
That I paid way too much
For these shoes
But every step I take
Reminds me that
They are three sizes too small

I shut down
I tighten every muscle
I scream inside my skull
I hold my breath
Until I die
I made another
Mistake

Frustration

The frustration runs
Deep and cold
The helplessness of humanity
Strangles my soul
I am silently losing
My breath
The coroner will list
The cause of death
Frustration

My wife
My soulmate
My best friend
Hell, my only friend
Constant victim
Of illness
Magnet for sorrow
Is tormented with pain
The kind of pain
That brings tears
To your eyes
And sounds to your lips
That are only vaguely human

It makes me regret
Never going to college
Never becoming a doctor
  Despite the fact that
  I faint at the sight of blood
I feel so helpless
Nothing I can do
Will ease the pain

Staying busy
To keep the brain
Occupied
Hamster on the wheel
Breaking a sweat
But accomplishing
Zero
I'm going nowhere
Fast

Wake up
At 3:45 AM
To a warmth on my arm
A lover's caress?
Or a serpent
Squeezing the life
Out of the prey?
Hair-trigger mind
Jumps to conclusions
Be prepared for the worst
So you'll never be disappointed

Frustration runs
Circles in vain
Helpless asleep
Even worse awake
I wish I could believe
But nothing seems to deserve
My belief

A Hate Crime?

I heard the news
Over the radio
At noon
On a jazz station:
Hate crimes
Are on the rise.

What exactly constitutes
A hate crime?

When two brothers
Use a shotgun
To erase their parents?
That's extremely hateful
And arguably
Criminal.

Although, I would be
Willing to bet
Those murders
Were not counted
As hate crimes.
Simply because
The assailants
And victims
Had the same colored skin.

The term puzzles
Me.
Aren't most crimes
And criminals
Hateful
Towards their victims
And themselves?

I suppose
Redneck crime
Or
Bigot crime
Or
Racially or religiously
Motivated acts of inhumanity
Wouldn't make great
Copy
In the news rooms.

Hate crime
It has a ring to it.

Back to Basics

I need help,
Yet I am
Beyond help.

I am afraid
Of failure,
Of your anger,
Of life itself.

I tiptoe
Through this mine field.
My serenity
Depends on
My ability
To save the world.

I've tied my tongue
In fear that I may
Blurt out
My feelings
Which may bring
A response
That I am not
Prepared to deal
With.

This is
The same poem
With different
Words.
Nothing has changed.
I've just learned
How to co-exist
With my problems.

I guess one could
Call that progress.

I break things
Less frequently,
Though I call myself
Stupid
More often.
Am I adjusting, accepting
Or simply
Holding it all in
Once again?

Whenever I speak up
I quickly come to
Regret it.

Tired of it all.
Back to basics.

Uncle Ray's Passing

Though it has been nearly
Twenty years
Since I have set
Eyes on the man,
Uncle Ray's passing
Knocked me back a step.

The connect-the-dot
Connection
From his stomach
Cancer
To my mother-in-law's
Breast
and bone
Cancer,
The mutual morphine,
The second-hand news
Over three thousand
Miles of fiber optic
Phone lines
Were a little too
Close to home.

Ray was a decent man,
  As far as I know.
    Aren't all uncles?
All I remember of him
Was that he was my cousins' father,
My aunt's husband
And he would walk
Around the block
After dinner.

All I remember
Was he took us
To some nameless
Faceless building
That he worked at
But it was the weekend
So the place was empty
And I still don't know what he did.

All I remember
Was we would stop at his house
  In Derry
On the way to my dentist
  In Manchester
So we could visit
  And so I could take my tranquilizer
But he was never home at the time.

His death reminds me,
  As Rita's did,
That someday my parents
Will be gone,
Their pedestals crumbled
Into tubes, painkillers,
EKG's, MRI's,
Catheters and surgeries,
More tragedy that I must prepare for.

I know more now than ever before:
He met my aunt while attending Fryeburg Academy.
He died at home refusing medical care.
He is buried next to my grandmother.

This Melancholy Dream

The rain
Drops onto the city
Dumping gloom
On the masses
My sadness seeps
Deeper
Into my psyche

Longing to walk
Through the rain
For hours

The falling water
Would erode my
Physical body
Dissolve my flesh
And run off
Into drains
Leading to the Pacific

Only my spirit
Would remain
Free of worldly
Obligations

Essence of a soul
Freedom in the wind
Peace

Longing to drive
Through the dark rain
For hours

Leaving worries
Several cities
Behind
Chasing serenity
Jazz wailing
Over the rhythmic downpour
Beating on my windshield

Why must the gas tank empty?
Why must the sun rise?
Why must the rain cease?

I yearn for this melancholy dream
To carry on

Death, Loss and the Overanalyzing Machine

People die. Another one dies every second, I'm sure. Strangers die. Some unnoticed, some on the evening news. It doesn't seem to have much effect on people. We all know we are all going to die, yet it doesn't seem real to us. Distant relatives die (usually when you are too young to comprehend) and pets die, but that isn't quite the same.

Death doesn't become real until it claims someone that you can't live without: your lover, your parents, your children, someone whose absence would truly make life no longer worth living. That's when death becomes real, when the warm body next to you in bed evaporates into a pile of cold, cold grief.

As far as I can determine, death punishes the survivors infinitely more than its victims. It chews away at our sanity, spitting out memories, attaching itself onto our weakest moments, leaching out our sorrow like a mosquito draining blood. Loss burns our spirit from the inside out, creating a sense of doom. Waiting for the next to go, and who that might be. Death whispers obscene threats into our psyche, warning us that our time is coming. When our own deaths are not sufficiently frightening, the loss of loved ones is dangled before our paranoid imaginations.

My wife is currently treading water in this ocean of death and loss. She mourns with each and every heart beat. Who could blame her? In the past two years she has lost her mother, grandmother, two pets, two next-door neighbors, numerous friends and countless acquaintances. She almost died giving birth to our son and was nearly killed in a car crash on Mother's Day. Death is no stranger to this woman.

As I observe my wife's grief, I am aware that one day, I too will wear that grief mask, dragging a fifty-pound weight around my heart, breathing becoming burdensome. I too will lose my parents, one at a time, no doubt, which will double the pain. I too will become an adult orphan.

My ultimate fear is not my own death. My ultimate fear is that one day I will lose her, the only one (save my son) whose absence would cut deep enough to cause implosion. As her life ends, "our life" will simultaneously dehydrate and dissolve before my eyes. The impossibility of facing another moment without her paralyzes me. This frightens me much more than my own death.

Yet this double-edged sword we call death is a crafty devil. If I am the one to go first (to put it gently) what I fear worse than my own death is leaving my wife to face the emptiness of life all alone. I picture her withered spirit crushed by losing a husband after countless previous tragedies. I see the violent grief ripping at her mind and soul. I would much rather bear the brunt of such pain than allow my wife to do so.

I guess that means I hope she dies first, which wasn't exactly what I meant. But that is what usually happens once I start my overanalyzing machine in motion. Nothing ever seems to turn out the way I intended it anyway.

2.

So as a child, what did *you* see
when you looked
in the mirror?

Vacant Lot

I am a vacant lot,
Empty and void
Of promise,
Totally without hope,
Darker than
When you close your eyes,
Darker than
A child molester's heart.

I am a vacant lot.
My futile attempts
At conversation
Crumble and fall
From my lips,
Leaving me waist deep
In quicksand secrets,
Choking on apprehension.

I am a vacant lot,
Incapable of embracing pleasure,
Crippled by self-hatred,
Twisted into submission
By my own delusions.
Your laughter scrapes
On my eardrums
And my mind begs for silence.

I am a vacant lot,
Stripped of value,
Purpose, reason,
Filled with discontent,
Unable to locate the
Shrapnel of my barren soul,
Nothing matters
At this precise moment.

I am a vacant lot.
I am not one of you.
I am from some other place.
Even those of you
That I like
I can barely tolerate.
It's no wonder
I have no friends
To speak of.

I am a vacant lot.
I am lost.
I am alone.
I am in pain.
I am nothing.
I am vacant.
I am a vacant man.
I am a vacant lot.

Fractured

It truly breaks my heart
watching you disintegrate
before my eyes.

Overwhelmed by stress
and lack of time,
rage becomes inevitable.

It pains me to observe
your bleeding spirit
lashing, flailing, screaming.

I've been there before,
in your shoes,
in your agony.

I remember the aching,
throbbing, desperate
strangle hold all too well.

Emotions constantly falling
through sudden, brutal
trap doors to misery.

Nothing mattered,
nothing sunk in,
during my harsh descent.

My only consolation
is knowing I survived
and am stronger for it.

Your path is littered
with endless, hidden,
land mine tragedies.

I can wrap you in my arms,
    if you'll let me.
I can tell you my story,
    if you'll listen.
I can lead you through this,
    if you'll follow.
I can help you,
    if you want.

Who am I fooling?

As much as I hate it
there's nothing I can do
to help you

except gather up the pieces
of your fractured sanity
and wait, and wait, and wait...

Tails, You Lose

Which half
Of this hell
Is more painful?

Watching a loved one
Wither
Riddled with tumors
That spread like
Small-town gossip

Struggling for life
Through countless
Surgeries
  Chemotherapy
   Morphine

The crippling pain
The paralyzing fear
The tortuous existence
For all involved

OR

The bittersweet
Memories of
Phone calls
  Recipes
   Shopping

The heartache
Of never
Being able to
Speak
With them again

The realization
That your son
Will never recall
The few months
He spent with
His grandma

Which is worse?

The anguish of
Watching your
Mother
Die

OR

The ache of
Living
Without her
After she is gone

The devil flips
A coin

Heads, I win
Tails, you lose

Brightest Star

Why must the brightest star
Burn out so soon?

Not some dead rock star
But a sweet, sweet woman
Whose smile still lights up photos

Why is she gone
  When others around her
  Linger on lifelessly?
Why is she gone
  While I am still here
  Taking up space
  Wasting oxygen?
Why is she gone
  Missing her grandson's
  Childhood?
Why is she gone
  Leaving a hole
  In our souls?
Why is she gone
  So soon,
    So soon?

Why do the brightest stars
Burn out so soon?

First Mass

Blessed Sacrament
Crucifixion murals
Rosary beads
Countless candles
Religious hierarchy
Bishops, Saints
The Pope
Symbolism deeply
Entrenched
In Catholic souls

Communion offered
By the priest
  God's mediator
And the peasants
Wait in line
  "This is my flesh
  Take of me"
As the baby
Suckles his
Mother's breast

Call and response
Ceremony
Worshippers recite
Memorized prayers
In unison
  "This is my blood
  Drink of me"
As the baby
Suckles his
Mother's milk

Darkness

"I was not fit for this world
and the this world was not fit for me."
– Charles Bukowski

The sky may be blue
  For now
And the clouds puffy
  And white
But this does not mean
My dark past
Is in my past

I sense I have
Gained a step
  Or two
On my dark side
My anger
  My fear
    My demons
And I am racing
Like hell
To maintain
That lead

One stumble
One mistake
And I could be
Swallowed whole
By my dark,
  Dark soul

Therapy led me
To a brighter
Viewpoint

But the danger
Remains
In my rearview
Mirror
Lurking like a bad
Detective
Always within sight

Will this dark
Cloud
Follow me to my grave?
Will this dark
Virus
Infect my son?
Will this dark
Ocean
Carry him away
To depression?
Will this darkness
Consume him as well?

Is it in my
Power
To destroy the
Darkness?

Countless

palm trees
cars
apartment buildings
hookers
streetlights
stop signs
languages
taxi cabs
religions
newspaper stands
bedroom windows
televisions
freeways
cell phones
banks
neckties
parking spaces
bars
broken hearts
  homes
    windows
aspiring actors
credit cards
illegal aliens
strip malls
crack houses
lost souls
cockroaches
gas stations
police cars
tourists
T-shirt vendors
homeless
runaways

busses
phone booths
balconies
sun glasses
murders
restaurants
musicians
churches
liquor stores
promises
stories
lies
disappointing
  frustrating
    failures
wife beaters
hungry children
garbage trucks
gang bangers
desperate people

A Note to My Child

You are still months away
from being born
and I can't wait
to see your eyes,
  mine?
your nose,
  mom's?
your smile.

Still unborn
yet you are the most
special,
loved and wanted
child in history.
Your mother and I
wished upon the stars
for you to be brought to us.

Words can not explain
the love I have for you,
more than every grain of sand
on every desert and every beach,
more than every wave of every sea
splashing on every grain of sand.

I love you more
than every baby ever born
to every mom and dad
throughout history,
more than all their fingers and toes,
all their eyes, ears and noses,
all their smiles, all their teeth
and every breath they ever took.

I love you
more than every star in the sky
and every mom and dad
ever wishing upon them
for every baby.
I love you this much
before ever holding you,
and I love you a little more every day.

Just wait until I see your smile
and I will love you even more still,
more than all the animals in the whole world,
more than all the birds, all the fish,
every cloud, every lake,
more than every man, woman, boy and girl
that ever lived, is alive now
or ever will live
forever.

061687 (2311)

Seclusion with a bottle
An easy way out
Or extra weight on my back?

Constantly searching
Never finding
Does that tell you anything?

Surrounded by lies
Can't help but becoming one myself
Living, breathing lie

One minute
All seems secure
In proper compartments

Then depression hits
Everything seems scattered
Words come out wrong

Life is funny that way
Constantly shifting
To keep you off guard

Depression

Depression
I once embraced it
As a long-lost guardian
Pleading for the security
Of insecurity.

At least I knew where I stood

Depression
I left it behind
Not as a prodigal son
But as a young adult moves
Into his first apartment.

Breaking the chains of childhood

Depression
I feel its cold grasp
On my entire being
Promising to take me back
To slow comfortable agony.

A second childhood or mid-life crisis?

Strangled by Stress

Got me by the balls this time
This ain't no nursery rhyme
No, buddy, I can't spare a dime
I'm up to my neck in this slime

Doing what I'm doing just to survive
At least I know that I'm alive
Spent a lifetime being deprived
Watch my ninth floor stage dive

Day-to-day bullshit trap
Does anybody have a map
I'm not swallowing this crap
Find another fool for that

Non-stop nervous breakdown
Take me to the lost and found
I damned near drowned
Too many inner scars to count

Calling out to the emptiness
I'm so sick of this
Feels like a boxer's fist
Is giving my skull a kiss

Strangled by stress
I confess
My brain is a mess

Inside the Cage

Inside the cage
In my mind
I have six views
Left
Right
Front
Back
Top
Bottom
Six shades of negative
Six shades of pessimism
Six lousy outlooks on life
So I close my eyes

And find a seventh shitty side!

The Good Boy

I once heard a wise man say
We will repeatedly be faced
With the same tests
Until we learn
The lesson meant for us.
I now see the depth of this truth.

As a boy
Growing up in an alcoholic environment
I was the adapter
I was the good boy
The tiny adult
Accepting responsibility
Forgoing childish fun.

I was searching for praise
Starving for appreciation
Following all the rules
Thinking that the good boys
Get all the rewards.
How I wrong I was.

My brother
The bad boy
Was always in trouble
Always getting attention.
The focus stayed on him.

I reached the crossroads
Of emotional paradox
I saw the attention going
To someone else
Someone who broke the rules
That I obeyed religiously.

I snapped, broke down
Inverted my beliefs
And self-destructed
Thirteen years of quicksand.

Today I saw a ghost
In the mirror
Here I am
A super husband
An expectant father
Waiting on my wife
Hand and foot
Cooking, cleaning, moving non-stop
Day in, day out
Never enough, never enough
  For me
The more I do
The more praise I deserve
Unfortunately it doesn't work that way.

What am I to learn from this?

Like a Man

I feel the guilt and shame
Crashing down
On me, the sinner
I see the sign posts
And I am miles
Backward from
Yesterday
The desert sun has baked
My skin to leather
And I sense nothing but pain
To the core of my soul

I am powerless
Before, during and after
Lying to myself
and my wife
Punching myself
In the face
Repeatedly

My mouth refuses
To say "no"
Or to admit
How sick I am

I'm on my knees
Weeping to a god
I told to go to hell
Twelve years ago

The scenery looks familiar
I swore I'd
Never
Return to this prison

Yet I walked in
Willingly
And swallowed the key

My eyes hurt
From having to look
At myself
Inside
Dark and scarred
Weak and incomplete
Self-loathing
Comes to mind
Self-hatred
Is more like it
Yet I can not wallow
In self-pity
I must walk on
Through the desert
Alone
Like a man

I am so scared

No Sense

There's a gridlock
Between my emotions and tongue
Gotta take a detour
Through paper and pen
Purge my mind of this confusion

Emotional handicap
Emotionally blind
No emotional wheelchair
No feeling eye dog
No Braille for the feeling
Impaired

No sense of smell
  Since I don't know when
No sense of emotion
  Since I don't know when

Calling out to you for a helping hand
Listen to my story
Ask the right questions
Then help me pick up the pieces
I still don't know if there are
Only a handful of large puzzle pieces
Or infinite shards of glass
Under the bare feet
Of a blind man

No sense of smell
No sense of emotion
No sense at all

I have to approach this disaster area
As an outsider solves a paradox

Analyze the issues, make some decisions
And clean up the mess

But there's more at stake
Than just my sanity
Nine years of joy and pain
Was it just a waste of time

I'm having a hard time lately
Making the sacrifice
Necessary to make a relationship work
Am I being selfish
Or focusing on the issue at hand

Once again I have to question
My motives
True love?
Easier than leaving?
Dependency?
Mother figure?

Maybe someday I'll know how I really feel
But that will just be one day's version
Of a gray subject
Not black and white
Some days I feel I have
No sense at all

Full Moon Friday

Role reversal
Full moon Friday
Liquor's off limits
For my own safety
And yours
  Trust me

Recreate the glamour
For the umpteenth time
Whatcha lookin' for this time?

No game plan
At least we abandoned the
One we had
A long time ago!

Weekends are full
Contact sports
With no teams
Just me against the world
And I'm pretty sure
I'm losing

Alternate extremes
Avoiding all clashes
Or creating them
Out of spite
Out of male molding
Thanks Dad
Thanks John Wayne

Spending my cash
On self-destruction
Spending my youth

In a fog of THC smoke
Creating a kinder
Gentler reality

Well I did it again
Exhausted dozens
Of empty lines
On blank paper
Trying to express
In English
My state of mind
In one frozen frame
In this motion picture of life

Eat Some Worms

Nobody likes me
Everybody hates me
Guess I'll go
Eat some worms

self-esteem:
  what you see
  when you
  look in the mirror

Looking back is scary
Remember the anguish
Children can be cruel
Yet children are fragile
Clay being molded
Before baking in the kiln
Locked into a permanent shape
A piece of art
Or an ashtray

SHRINK:
So as a child, what did *you* see
when you looked in the mirror?

CLIENT:
I saw a kid who wasn't worth
meeting, getting to know or liking.

Formative years have gone
Dice have been rolled
Learned from my environment
I was worthless
  Everyone is
Emotions are a waste of time

So now you wonder
Why I still hate the world

I don't like anybody
I hate everyone
Why don't you all
Eat some worms

My Skull is Crushing

My skull is crushing
Inward
From external pressure
Out of my control
Over analyzing
Shit that doesn't matter

My skull is crushing
Outward
From internal pressure
Can't control my own head
Over analyzing
Everything I set my mind on

My skull is crushing
Me
Runaway emotions
Running my everyday life
One way or another
I've got to let go

My skull is crushing
You
I know I'm not
The easiest guy to live with
Before I chase you away
I've got to let go

My skull is crushing
My soul
The one I denied for so long
My insides feel
Like root canal without Novocain
I don't dare to let go

My skull is crushing
Spinning, tearing, shredding
Everything in sight
Self-destruction
As an art form
I don't know how to let go

Wash Away the Pain

Woman, I have such respect
and empathy
for the cross you bear
silently.
The last few days
have come crashing
across your shoulders.
The weight of the world
that I sometimes attempt to carry
seems light as a feather
next to your burden.

Losing the gift
of all gifts,
the seed of life that is your nature,
the blessing you have
wished for,
snatched away,
promise broken,
along with your heart.
A tidal wave of questions:
"Why me?"
"What did I do wrong?"
"Will I ever have a child?"

Life, with its brutal mercy,
gave you a few days
to catch your breath,
dry your tears
and get back on your feet,
before punching you in the gut,
knocking the wind from your soul.

The woman who bore you
is yet again scratching
and clawing for her life.
Poison spreading,
corroding her body
and spirit,
dragging her down
to the point of submission.
You, the seed of her love,
are trapped between
two tragedies:
your mother
and your child.

Three thousand miles apart
from the one needs you.
Tears have flowed
but I doubt a lifetime of tears
would wash away the pain.

Like Looking in the Mirror

I see your anguish
and it breaks my heart.
I understand the pain
like looking in the mirror.
Your body shakes
with the overwhelming
hurt, fear
and anger
built on a foundation
of an abused child.

I recognize the tears
falling in short bursts.
Spring showers,
but no thunder storms.
Can't seem to release
the flood gates,
open the dam.
Too much pain
for one soul to bear.

I sense the helplessness
of life
and the 11 o'clock news
depressing even the
eternal optimist.
Trapped in the middle
of a withering mother
and an invisible child,
your back is breaking
under the weight of
your world.

I've felt the pain
so deep
you can't find words.
Blackness snowballs
bigger every day
total eclipse of the soul.
All I can do
is hold you near
and catch your tears
with my shoulder.

I hope you find
some relief
and peace of mind.
I feel like I'm
looking in the mirror
and it hurts like hell!

Je t'aime.

3.

The night is growing longer, darker, colder

In Memory of Rita MacKay

I met Rita 12 years ago when I started dating her daughter. She was as over protective as any mother of a 17-year-old girl would be. Yet through time we became very close.

If you ever want to see a glimpse of the impact or worth of a person's life, you only need to look at their children. As anyone who knows this family could tell you, Lori and Rob are two of the most loving, caring and giving people you will ever meet. This says a great deal about the example Rita set for them.

It is often said that a person's actions speak louder than their words. It is extremely easy to declare that you have certain values or beliefs. But how many of us act accordingly?

Rita MacKay was a survivor. For many years, she fought a disease that takes most of its victims in a matter of months. Yet she did more than survive during those years. She refused to let her disease take away her life. Inevitably, it took her physical body, but she refused to stop living simply because she was sick. She always had a smile on her face. In fact, speaking with Rita on the phone, I could hear the smile in her voice. She was determined to squeeze as much enjoyment out of her time on this Earth as possible. I never heard her use the phrase "Life is too short," but she lived it every day.

Rita visited us in Los Angeles several times including a 3-week stay to meet her new grandson earlier this year. Every time she came to visit, she was going non-stop. She wanted to experience all that our city had to offer. She walked along Venice Beach and the Hollywood Walk of Fame. She shopped the garment district for bargains, and drove around looking for yard sales.

Rita didn't let anything hold her back. She joined us in a nightclub and danced well into the night. She went up to famous musicians and asked them to pose for pictures with her. She gave cigarettes and money to homeless panhandlers. She always spoke her mind and she always enjoyed herself.

Everyone here will hold a set of mental images or snapshots in their hearts of how they remember Rita. I will always recall her smile, her laugh and her loving spirit. But the one picture I will always cherish is her rocking my son to sleep, singing a lullaby.

Alexandria

I hope that
One day
You see
Your parents
For who
and what
They really are.

I hope you'll see
All your mother
Has done for
You.
All she has
Sacrificed,
All she has
Endured,
For your benefit.

I hope you'll
Appreciate
The meals she
Struggled
To provide
And prepare.

I hope you'll
Understand
What it takes
For a woman
To raise a child
Alone.
Then again,
I pray you never
Have to find out
What that is like.

I hope you'll
Realize
Just why she was
Alone,
Why your father
Was never around.

I hope you
Can place
The blame
Where it belongs,
On your father's
Shoulders.

He couldn't accept
Responsibility
Or reality.
He couldn't control
Himself,
Yet insisted on
Controlling others.

He didn't understand
That three meals a day
Were more important
Than a Disney video
Every few months
Or a trip
To Chuck E. Cheese's.

He didn't comprehend
That discipline
Comes before
Special treats.

He doesn't even know
The meaning
Of the word
Love,
Which isn't totally
His fault,
But it sure as hell
Isn't yours.

Be grateful
Your mom
Has shown,
Through her own example,
What love looks like
And how it feels.

Don't blame yourself
For your Dad's
Shortcomings.
It's his life
That needs
Fixing,
And until he is willing
To do what's necessary,
Nothing will change.
He'll just keep
Running in place,
In the same
Dark, miserable
Place.

Never forget
That I love you,
And Roqsi loves you,
And Drake loves you.
You can count
On us.

I am so sad
That you didn't have
A dad
You could lean on
And be loved by.
I wish I could
Fill
That void
But I can't.
No one can.

Take strength
In the fact
That your mom
And Roqsi
Both grew up
Without their dads too.
You can overcome,
You can learn
From their
Example.

Please don't assume
All men are
Irresponsible
And will hurt you.
I hope
I have never
Hurt you.
There are good
And bad
Men
And women.

Grow up
To be a good woman
And find a good man.
Don't look for

A replacement
For your father.
Don't try to
Fix a bad boy.
Find a man
Who will show you love
And stick around
For your
Children.

I know life
Isn't fair.
I know this hurts.
But I am always
Here for you.

Gauntlet

How long can I
Hold my
Breath
Bite my
Tongue
Bridle my
Simmering
Spiteful
Rage?

I constantly find
Myself
Trapped
In smothering
Circumstances,
Walls closing in,
Authority's
Hot breath
On my neck,
The vice around
My balls
Squeezing tighter
By the day.

At first
I selflessly
Adapt
To my environment,
No matter how
Unpleasant
Or downright
Unbearable.
I close my eyes,
Plug my nose,

And belly flop
Into the ocean
Of bullshit.

After a period of time,
Generally a few months
That seem to last
Several lifetimes,
My patience
Evaporates into
Resentment
That feels like a
Fifty-pound weight
Around my ankle.
I would contemplate
Amputating
My foot
Before leaving
The stifling situation.

I mumble
Curses, insults
And vow to end
My misery;
Only to replace it
With an equally
Horrific
Existence.

Time begins to
Drag.
Days turn into
Years.
  Dog years.
Battery acid churns
In my gut,
Poisoning
My emotions,

My thought patterns,
Crippling
My sanity,
My serenity.

Just as I come
To grips
With the reality
Of my situation,
Accept its difficulty,
Swallow
And move on,
Another level of
Crap
Is dropped
On my head,
In my lap,
As if to test
My willpower.
Increased demands
Turn it up a notch,
Tighten the vice,
Whisper in my ear
  "I'll get you."
   "Can you take it?"
   "You're gonna fail."

After centuries of
Ulcers,
Migraines
And divorces,
I discover
Myself in a paradox:
I am still unable
To walk away,
Sever my ties
To this hell;
Yet I am now unable

To withstand the torture
That my masochistic
Side thrives on.
The martyr is no longer
Willing to suffer
In vain.

I begin to act
Like a different man,
An angry man,
A violent man,
A man on the verge
Of a breakdown
Or a breakthrough.

I confront my oppressors
With hostility,
Unleashing a bottomless
Pit of filth.
I get in screaming
Matches
Where I have nothing
To gain
Except pride
  Or release,
And much
Too much
To lose.

I teeter on the edge,
Knowing full well
That sooner or later
I will fall off
The balance beam
Into the unknown

As I survey
The wreckage,
The aftermath,
I ponder
What lesson
I am to learn
From being constantly
Led through this
Gauntlet.

Is it to learn
How to persevere
In the face of turmoil,
How to suck it up
And carry on
Despite
Difficulties?

Or am I to realize
That I must avoid
These situations
Altogether?

Or is that
Simply
Quitting?

This Dark and Lonely Path

I have been down
This dark
And lonely path
Once before.
It seems like
Last week
I shuffled
With head hung
Low,
Eyes locked on
This dusty road to
Hell,
Feet dragging
Through dry
Withered leaves.

My heart weighed
Twenty pounds
Sluggishly beating
Inside my rib
Cage,
Wishing for it all
To simply
End.

The numbness
Of thought,
The painful
Reminders
Of doom,
Inevitable
Doom.

Lying awake at night,
Waiting for sleep.
Crying for answers,
Praying for answers,
Begging for answers.
Answers that
Thousands have
Pleaded for,
Answers that
Will never
Come.

The whirlpool,
The quicksand,
The magnetic pull
Of sadness,
Depression,
Anger,
Hopelessness,
Oh God, the hopelessness.

The night is growing
Longer,
Darker,
Colder.

The pain
Has come
Full circle.
Is this the
Beginning
Or the end?
Will it
Ever end?

One of Those Days / Nights

Mama never said
There would be
Days like these

The day
Someone burned
The covered bridge
In Redstone, NH
I stood looking
Over the river
Full of embers
Awed by the
Separation
Of two sides
Of land

The day my Bible
School teacher
Left his wife
And two daughters
To marry a
Seventeen-year-old
Girl
From the Bible study
That I had a crush on

The day
The marshals
Evicted us
At six AM
Putting us on the street
With two dogs
Because we would rather
Party than pay rent

The night I got
The shit kicked
Out of me
By at least twenty people
At the Soul House party
Over a drug dealer
Stealing a can of beer

The night Eric
Was arrested
For drunk driving
In my car
And my father
Had to get me
Out of jail

The night
(Thanksgiving '85)
That our apartment
Burned to the ground
Before our eyes

Etc., etc., etc.

Mama never said
There would be
Nights like these

Medgar Evars

I can not fathom
The strength it takes
To be a civil rights
Leader,
To be a fearless
Voice
Against the wind of oppression.

I can not fathom
The evil
That would lead someone
To murder another man,
To shoot that man
In the back,
In front of his
Wife
And children,
Leave him to die
In their arms.

All because
That man's
Skin
Had a different
Pigmentation
Than yours.

All because
You do not view
A black man
As a man at all,
And that is more difficult
To comprehend
Than murder itself.

Lincoln's
Blood-stained
Face
On a five-dollar bill.

A poll tax receipt
Covered in
Medgar Evar's
Blood.

The silence I hear
Is a world mourning
  or ignoring
Another victim,
Another lost hero,
  Husband,
    Father.

Lost Eyes

Eyes that weep
  Without tears
Eyes that speak
  Of lifelong sorrow
Eyes that whisper
  Secrets that
The heart doesn't
  Even know.

Past pain
Splashing
In the dark cold water
Of a silvery lake.
Swimming,
Or simply trying
Not to drown.
Kicking, thrashing,
Swallowing water
As you scream for
Mercy.

Waking startled
From an isolation
Nightmare
Only to realize
Real life
Isn't much better,
  Sometimes it's
  Even worse.

You've lost
All you were born
Into,
All that came before

You,
Your family tree,
Roots and all.

Lost eyes
  Bottomless pit of pain
Lost eyes
  Avoiding everything and everyone
Lost eyes
  Spreading the hurt with your glare
Lost eyes
  Distant, distant, distant….

Flu

I feel the flu
Coming on,
Coming from a distance.
I feel it
Coming closer,
Long before
The achy body,
The swollen sinuses,
The cough,
The miserable,
Terrible,
Physical symptoms
Arrive.

I feel myself
Acting
And reacting
Differently.

I have no energy,
No desire
To accomplish
Anything.
Multiple choice
Options
Perplex me.
I walk away
Shaking my
Foggy head.

I'm edgy.
I want something
And detest it
When it lands

In my lap.
I want space,
But feel lonely.
I'm hungry
But bothered
With decisions
Of what to eat.
I snap at
My wife,
My son,
Strangers,
The TV.

I want to sleep
For days.
I go to bed
Before 9,
Wake at 6,
Wishing I had
Two more hours.
I yawn and
Start my day
Again.

At the office
I stare
At my work
In a daze.
How does this stuff
Function?
How do I
Do this?
What should I
Tackle first?
My God,
This job is stifling
Me
And I wasn't

Even aware
Of it.

I walk the dog
At night,
Before going to bed
So very early.
I get the urge
To drive
Anywhere,
For hours.
Watching the stars,
Pondering
Life.
Yet, when I return
Inside
I'd rather sleep
Than drive.

I forgo
The night job,
Calling in
"Sick"
Before I really am
Because I can't
Fathom
Four hours
Of that
Crap.

Yet when
It really hits,
And I know it
Will,
I won't be able
To call in
Due to economic
Reasons.

I'll have to
Trudge along
In my sinus-induced
Misery,
Hating every minute
Of it.

I feel the flu
Coming on.

Flux

We have all heard how
Nothing remains the same
Everything is in a constant
State of flux
Perpetual change
You can't stand still
You're either moving forward
Or backward
You either get better
Or worse
But never stay the same
Etc., etc., etc....

So the question is simple
Which direction
Are you going in?
Forward?
Or backward?

Do you reach out
 to others?
Do you embrace
 people and moments?
Do you lend a hand?
 or pull it away?
Do you turn your back?
 your cold, cold shoulder?
Do you walk away?

Do you stand up
 for what's right?
Do you close
 your jaded eyes?

Do you run for daylight?
  or from your demons?

Do you strive to make
  things better around you?
Do you throw gasoline
  on the forest fire?

Do you work for peace?
Or do you polish your gun, waiting?

Which direction
Are you moving in?

How Much Can a Man Take?

this life seems to consist of
one maddening ordeal
after another
mercifully separated
by stretches of calm
before storms

those down times are excruciating
the pressure can destroy a man
pulverize him
crush him into an empty shell
stripped of all hope

a soul can only withstand
so much pressure
it's a matter of physics
everything has a breaking point
triggers waiting to be squeezed

how much can a man take?
some more than others

some snap at a simple look
from a spouse or stranger
some can survive holocausts
others can withstand physical
and mental anguish
we all have a different
threshold of madness

lack of parking spaces?
the ticking clock?
financial nightmares?
starving children in China?

cancer that crouches
in a tree
behind a rock
inside a pack of cigarettes
surrounding you with asbestos
walls covered in lead paint
preying on your family
eliminating one at a time
until only you are left
only then will you know
fear with no boundaries

how much can a man take?
you're about to find out

Down, Down, Down

I've chased demons
and negative thoughts
from the corners of my skull.

I've swept them away
like piles of accumulated
dust, dirt and general filth.

I've fumigated detrimental
emotions from the recesses
of my bleak soul.

I've worked harder on this
than just about anything
in my three-plus decades.

I've followed directions,
done and abstained from
all the right things.

I've seen the rewards
of these efforts in a much
more positive frame of mind.

Yet lately, I've been feeling
down for the first time
since I can recall.

Not your run of the mill
sad about stuff
that would make anyone sad.

Not the devastating
but perfectly normal grief
after losing a loved one.

But deep down to the bone
pain, waiting for me as I
wake every single day.

Those angry at the world,
wish I'd never been born,
where's the escape hatch blues.

Lately I've been circling
the proverbial drain,
closing in on despair.

Hating myself and my life,
taking every opportunity
to kick me when I'm down
  down
    down.

Broken Heart

As the father
of an intelligent
young boy,
who is part Native American,
I have many questions
to answer before
he asks them;
and he will.

When his mother
refuses to stand
for the national anthem,
a song celebrating this country,
stolen from her people
by ruthless, greedy murderers,
how do I explain this to my son?

How do I explain
being Mic Mac is more
than dancing to the drum
at an occasional pow wow?
How do I explain
the past?
the genocide?
the pain?
How do I begin
to explain?

How does one promote
heritage without
discussing the oppressors,
which happen to be
my forefathers,
and sadly,
his also?

When this leads him to pride
in his native ancestry,
how do I,
as a white man
handle his new found disgust
for white men?

When he realizes his blood
is more white
than red,
how do I help him
through the confusion,
the anguish,
self-doubt,
self-hatred?

After all he is more
of what he will detest
than what he will embrace?

How will we progress
to a point where
the past is the past,
a man is a man
and a broken heart
is a broken heart?

No more,
no less.

How Do You Sleep at Night

What tangled
Set of lies
Do you sell
Yourself
While you are awake
That allows you
The peace of mind
Required
To actually
Sleep at night?

Because if I
Were you
I'd be an insomniac
Never once could I
Catch a catnap
Not even a second

How do you
Excuse
The filth
That comes out
Of your mouth,
The damage
You spread to those
Around you,
The poison
That you eat,
Breathe, sweat,
Piss and shit?

Because if I
Were you
I'd have to resort

To heavy
Pharmaceuticals
Or suicide
Just to stop
The spinning
Burning
Maddening
Self-hatred machine
From shredding
My nights
Into desperate hours
Of emotional quicksand
Sucking me deeper
Into my hellish
Obsessions

No way out
None whatsoever

How do you
Sleep
At night?

Repeating the Cycle

STOP!
Look what you are doing
You are becoming
Your father

- - -

Despite extreme effort
And intense introspection
I am repeating the cycle
I am letting
My anger
Get the best of me

I grip, I press
　Slow down
I stress myself out
　Have patience
I try to control
This little soul
　Just let him be
　A two-year-old

My temper
My anger
Burns with the slightest
Spark
Forest fire's fury
In a flash

My voice booms
My face contorts
I see the fear
In my son's face

Too late
To take it back
Too late
To erase the memory
Is it too late?

Despite my sacrifices
Despite my therapy
Despite my tendency
Towards martyrdom
My son will grow up
In fear
Of me
Of my rage
If I don't stop
The pattern
If I don't break
The circle
If I don't stop
Repeating the cycle

Somewhere

It's all happening
Right now
As you read this
Anything you could
Think of
Is happening
Somewhere

Somewhere
It's raining
Somewhere
It's snowing
Somewhere
The wind is blowing
Probably even a
Hurricane
Somewhere

Somewhere
It is dawn
Somewhere
Dusk
It is midnight
Noon
Even 4:00 PM
Somewhere

Kids at school
Thieves in the silent
Night
Couples creating more
Babies for the next
Generation

A farmer is milking
Cows
While the stock boy
Puts more gallons
On the shelves
While children
Pour it on
Their cereal
All at once
Somewhere

A man is killed
Over drug money
A martyr over
His beliefs
Writers write
Readers read
Fascists censor
And burn books
All at once
Somewhere

Somewhere
Drunks are brawling
In a greasy alley
Birds greet the dawn
With their joyous
Ignorant songs
Joy from the sunlight
Rising for another day
Ignorant of all the evil
We humans inflicted
During the darkness

People are praying
To various gods:
Christ
Allah

Buddah
Satan
And the current
Cult leader
Of the week

Spinsters are saving
Nickels in coffee cans
While high rollers
Go for broke
In neon, polyester
Hell

Crickets chirping
Cars crashing
Prophets preaching
To tourists
Who walk away
Shaking their heads

Oceans glisten
In the tropical sun
Carry cruise liners
Full of senior citizens
Harbor sharks
And sunken ships
And mobsters
With cement slippers
Drown innocent swimmers
Throw tidal waves on
Unsuspecting islands

Somewhere
Children are reading
Sleeping
Starving
Dodging bullets
Walking the streets

Trading sex
For shelter

Somewhere
A baby is born
Somewhere
A sick man dies
Somewhere
Birth, life and death
Co-exist
In uneasy chaos

Somewhere
An old man
Ponders
His carefree childhood
Somewhere
A young boy
Daydreams
About manhood's freedoms
Somewhere
A homeless man
Begs for his
Next meal

Somewhere
Everywhere
People are choking
On their self-centered
Anguish
Right now

Somewhere
Sometime
Someone
Will unlock
Life's mysteries
But that sometime
Is not now

Somewhere
Someone
Is happy
But that someone
Is not me

Somewhere
There is peace
But that somewhere
Is not here

Three Dollars

Humid night
Outside Ralph's
Supermarket
Homeless couple
With homeless
Child

Break my heart
Break my soul
Break my willpower
Break my own rules

Spare change for
Milk, diapers, room
For the night
  I've heard it before
My husband has a job
He just hasn't gotten
Paid yet
  I've heard it before
  I've heard it all
  Before

  Forget the homeless
  Adults
  Mute out their
  Self-pitying words
  Block out their
  Too sincere faces

If anyone reports us
As homeless
We will lose our child
They will take our son
Away

Unable to shop
Unable to focus
Unable to think
Unable to simply forget

I hand them
Three dollars
And hope the money
Doesn't go to booze
Or crack
I hand them
Three dollars
And pray the boy
Survives this ordeal
And rises
Above

My son on the streets?
My son without food?
My son in a foster home?
My son, my poor, poor son….

There but for
The grace of God
Go I

Rain

For years
My wife has been the one
In love with
Rain

  This is my type of day
  She would proclaim

The gray skies
Brought out her
Romantic side
The humidity would
Release into a
Glorious downpour
That cleansed
The sky,
Leaving the world
A brighter place

  This is my type of day
  She would proclaim

While I detested
The inconvenience
The slippery roads
The sneezing and sniffling
The delayed baseball games
The halt of normality

However, I have noticed
That lately
I found the rain
Pleasing
To my melancholy soul

I picture the water
Washing away
My worries
Rinsing my flesh
From my bones
Allowing my spirit
To float through
The rain clouds
To escape

I sleep soundly
And my dreams
Are not chaotic
Or anxiety ridden

I enjoy walking
In the rain
And would continue
For hours
If not for fear
Of pneumonia

This is my type of day
She would proclaim

Sadness

The last sip
Of your last beer
The last drag
Of your last
Cigarette
The last cent
To your name
The final day
Of summer vacation.

Sadness is
The last taste
Of a good thing
That you knew
All along
Was about to run out
So you couldn't even
Enjoy it
Because the end
Of the line
Was staring you down.

Just as the sun
Begrudgingly
Recedes to the west
Gripping the horizon
Refusing to release
The day.

Misery

I've sensed
The difference
Between
Being weighed down
By stress,
The straight jacket
Of no options
No solutions
No way out
Of this hole,
Constant dependency
To a drug
A job
A mate
A state of mind.

And the weightlessness
Of freedom
When you
Let go
Of preconceived
Notions.
Such ecstasy,
Too bad
It doesn't last
More than a few seconds
Before the quicksand
Sucks you back
Down
To the depths of
Misery.

Regret

Black smoke
On a gray
Gloomy day
Oil refinery
Burning
On a rainy day

Push and shove
Ricochet emotions
Escalating
To the point
Of anger

Insults, snarls
Threats and tears
Tapestry of sadness
Woven
On top of
Thirteen years
Of love

Broken hearts
Can mend
If that is what
Both halves
Truly desire

Polar opposites
Push and pull
Force their will
Only see things
From their side
Of the fence

Struggle
Resistance
Resentment
Revolt

Where does this lead us?
Where does this leave us?

Oh my poor soul
Hurts
When we fight
Yet it also hurts
When my view
Can not be expressed
Accepted
Approved

Where does this lead us?
Where does this leave us?

Regret
That's where it leads

4.

I can't forgive. I can't forget

Black Blood

Here I go again
Same shit different day
My black heart pumping
Black blood
Throughout my body
And soul

Keeping all those
Black feelings
On the inside
Recirculating through my body
Keeping my outlook on life
Black as a moonless night

Avoiding expression
Like a hemophiliac
Avoids a paper cut
I can't afford to lose a drop of
Black blood

Anger, fear, frustration,
Insecurity, inferiority,
Rage, shame, self-hatred,
Suicidal fantasies

Black blood in my veins

Those Eyes

Outer shell
A macho facade
Swagger, spit, self-centered
Soldier, cowboy, All-American boy next door
Superman

But....
Look deeper into
Those eyes
And you will see the same animal

Scared shitless
Like a deer in the path
Of a pair of headlights
That brings an end to it all

Afraid of
Not fitting in
Rejection
Being the center of attention
Or not

Those eyes bleed fear
Low self-esteem
All those hidden male characteristics

Avoid the Human Race

I've taken two steps forward
So where's the three steps back
I've come to expect
Patiently waiting 'til my
Attention fades
Leaving the naked self-esteem
Vulnerable
To mindfucking sirens
To ego crushing dickheads
And any religion
Promising peace of mind
At any cost

I've noticed a pattern
In the puzzle of my life
No matter where I stood
In church or insane
In the back seat during a blizzard
No matter what the pain
Or pleasure I always chose to
Avoid the human race

(Is this my "problem"
or just another theme
For a support group?)

My Emotional Minefield

While you're at it
Girl
Could I persuade you
To piece together
The jigsaw puzzle
In my skull
Only I'm not quite
Sure
How many pieces
You're looking for
I lost count before I met you

Hope you're up to this challenge
Girl
It's not like those cartoon mazes
I didn't come with a picture
To guide you
No rhyme or reason
No holds barred
No time outs
No second chances
My emotional minefield

Who's to Blame?

Who's to blame
when you miss the bus
and arrive thirty minutes late
for a job interview,
only to discover
the job has been filled?

Who's to blame
when nations commit murder
over oil, money
and spiritual preference,
training millions of men
to kill each other?

Who's to blame
when your Sunday school teacher
leaves his family
to marry
a seventeen
year old blond
that you have a crush on?

Who's to blame
when alcoholism
runs in your family,
countless generations
with no beginning to the
vicious drunken cycle?

Who's to blame
when your mother develops
a cancerous tumor
the size of a tennis ball
pushing through her flesh

as she lights another
cigarette?

Who's to blame
when life hurts,
but it's nobody's fault,
so you swallow
the burning pain
and hold your breath?

What's Stopping Me?

I refuse
to recover.
  I push away
  the entire world.
I deny
there is a problem.
  I pound my head
  against the wall.
I look out from my
  voluntary
solitary confinement
that shuts them out
while locking me in.
  Social skills of a rock.
  How to lose friends
  and isolate people.
I spent months
untying the knots
that strangled my soul,
  only to trip
  over the rope
  I was hanging myself with.
Will I ever escape
  my "self"?

My arms are crossed
folded in front of me.
  A sign to the world
  "Give me space."
My mouth is full
of food and drink,
  stuffing down
  all those emotions.

My brain is in
self-destruct mode,
  freak show mirror
  that reflects only flaws.
My nerves are frayed,
exposed to the elements,
  bleeding and raw,
  numbed by the pain.
My heart is silent,
shattered to dust.
  All the therapy and
  super glue won't help.
My head is aching,
tired of questions,
  self-doubts
  and infinite mazes.

So Much to Ask

When will I learn
I can't carry your world
On my shoulders,
I can't solve the Rubik's cube
Of my emotional maze,
I can't do everything
All at once,
When will I learn?

All the advice I am hearing
Is easier said
Than done.
Hell, I don't understand
Half of it.
  "Don't let it bother you."
  "Let it roll off your back."
  "Find something to do with your anger."
What do these things
Mean?

All I know
Is I want to protect
My wife
From the world,
Whatever it takes.
Is that
So much to ask?

I'm Sad and Angry

I'm sad
That your mother
Is so ill,
That I haven't seen you
Or our son
For months,
That I miss you so,
That I am losing
Valuable, precious
Moments
Of our new family.

I'm angry
That you can see Drake
Grow and change
And do those cute baby things
That I will never see.
I know I will have you both
For many years
But I will never see his first tooth
Or him crawling for the first
Time.

I'm sad and angry
That once again
Other people's needs
Come before mine.

Fear of Faith

My soul
Opened to a familiar
Yet prodigal
Sense of peace
Only to be slammed
Shut
Like a coffin
Complete
With hammer
And nails

I could smell
The peace
The serenity
The security
Frozen
In fifteen
Years of Novocain
Thawing

Oyster's shell
Opening
Pearl
Within sight

Fear of faith
Choking me
I step back
Shut the door
Close my heart
And mind
Yet the image remains
On the back side
Of my eyelids
I've been here before

Oh God
I was so happy
Before
My heart was ripped from
My soul

I can't forgive
I can't forget

I STILL HATE YOU!

Last Friday

Last Friday
Scared the hell out of me.
Almost lost my child
Whom I had never met.

Driving to the hospital
Between tears
And screams
  "Fuck you, God!"
Disbelief
That our baby could be
Taken away
Erased from our existence
Before I could even
See the beautiful face.

Fear
Of losing control
And losing
The one thing I wanted
With all my heart.

Worrying about
The mother of the child
My wife
My soul mate
Hospitalized for the
First time.

Sleepwalking through
The weekend
Moving to our new
Empty home
Sleeping alone

Wondering what
Has been lost,
Taken away.

Relief
That our baby
Is healthy
Only a
Threatened miscarriage
A warning.

A path of eggshells
Is before me
And the world is on my back.
Which will crumble first
The eggshells
Or me?

The tortoise keeps crawling
Oblivious to the weight
Accumulating on its shell.
The world is a monkey
On my back.

Knee Deep

Knee deep
In 120-degree sand
For weeks
Horizon offers nothing
But more sand
As far as the eye can see
More burning sand
In my eyes
In my soul

Focus on the moment
One day at a time
The big picture
Would crush my heart

Life
With all its complexities
Can be nearly as brutal
As death
Which is the ultimate
Brutality
Even when merciful

In losing Rita
The world is losing
A mother
Grandmother
And mother-in-law

As well as
A wife
Daughter
Sister
And probably

A cousin
And aunt
Several times over

Not to mention
A very good
Friend

Lost, Lonely, Insecure and Frightened

Why do I feel
Like an egg
That's been dropped
Smashed on the floor
Infinite pieces of shell
Some large
  Some small
Some scattered in the corner
Never to be seen
Insides leaking
All over the linoleum
A sticky, slimy mess?

Why do I feel
Like an accident
Waiting to happen?
A time bomb ticking?
The sock lost in the laundry
  Eight months ago?
A blind stray dog
Who's been kicked and burned?
A bolt of lightning
In the open sea?

Why do I feel
Lost, lonely, insecure and frightened?

Non-Existence

For years now,
Whenever life got me down,
When I couldn't take anymore
Pain,
My attention went towards
Death.
Why was that?
Death is the opposite of life
  (Right?)
And life is painful
  (Right?)
What's a depressed alcoholic to do
But end it all?

But the light bulb
Went on today.
Life and death are not opposites.
They are siamese twins
Joined at the hip.
One leads to the other;
A beginning to an end.
You can't be dead unless
You have once been alive.
You would just be unborn.

What I was really thirsty for
Was to have never been born,
Unliving, undead,
Non-existence.

Gone (Soothing Presence)

Eyes dimming
Closed lids
Swept into darkness
Approaching sleep
When it hit
Me:
You are
Gone.

Seven weeks
Drifted like snow
Into the
Past.

Your mother needs
You and your
Soothing presence
For comfort in her
Final days,
So you and our
Six-month-old son are
Gone.

I can no longer
Numb
The throbbing ache
That crushes my chest
When I realize
What has been stolen
From me.

I have been waiting
For my son's
First tooth,

First step,
First words
And God forbid
His first Christmas.
Time I can never
Replace.

I have such an
Addiction
To your soothing
Presence
To get me through
Life's shit storms.

I can barely remember
The sensation of
Holding you,
Your laugh,
Our son's squeal
Of delight.
They are all
Gone.

I know I will
Get you both
Back.
And I know there are bigger
Issues than my loneliness,
But this burns my soul
And begs to be expressed.

My "Self"

Digging deep
Deeper than ever before
Down to the buried treasure
My "self"
A smiling boy
Stuck in a time lock
Left behind
By an angry young man
Jaded from years of
Emotional solitude

Ready to reach
Farther than ever before
Across the divide
Between me and my "self"
Tearing down the wall
Brick by brick
And bridging the canyon
Created to protect my "self"
From the unbearable pain

Tired of "self" destruction
And the toll on my
Soul
The anesthesia no longer
Kills the pain
My own worst enemy
Is in the mirror
And he's the only one
Laughing at me

Layer by layer
The onion peels
Exposing my "self"

Without shame
Take the world
Off my shoulders
Start trusting
In life itself
And raise
My "self" esteem

Low Tolerance

In case you haven't noticed
I have a low tolerance
Lately
For the shit storm
Life dumps on me

If I act like a child
It's due to the deep
Digging
Into my past
Resurrecting buried pain
Investigating the crime
Solving the mystery
Reliving
The living hell
Feeling that empty
Crushed
Paralyzing
Hurt
That overwhelmed me
To the point of shutting down
Shutting off my heart
And soul

Be patient with me
This is only temporary

I've been through
This part of town
Before
Just on a different street
I'll find my way back
With a smile in my heart
And in my soul

As soon as I take care
Of business
I have a few more
Stops to make
Scores to settle

If my wounded
Inner child is showing
Please be patient with me
This is only temporary

What doesn't kill me
Will make me stronger

Family Portraits

Women with twisted,
hollow faces that
wince and moan
from a life that
became painful.
Showing off
their suicide scars
like a new
pair of shoes
or a midsummer tan.

Men with weary,
desperate eyes that
whisper secret heartaches,
scream at life's futility,
but never sing a joyful tune.
Wearing their burdens
like a martyr's cross
or a badge of honor.

Children with a
convict's stare,
suspicious of silence
and empty promises.
Removing splinters of trust
from their anorexic hearts
as if defusing a bomb.

You may not
be able
to judge books
by covers,
but you can
sure as hell

read people's
faces.

Celebrities with artificial,
cheekbone smiles.

Policemen with callused,
granite frowns.

Janitors with that silent,
lock jaw glare.

Single mothers with tear
streaked mascara.

And me, with my
head hung low.

Grampa

Grampa used to sit
on his porch nearly
every spring and summer
  and occasionally fall
evening
listening to Red Sox games
on the radio
  this was before cable TV
even the West Coast games
with 10 o'clock starts
that went well past midnight
keeping meticulous box scores
  hits, runs and errors
162 times per year
even doubleheaders.
He saved every last one
beside the full color
team photo
that came free
in the *Manchester Union Leader*
once a year
during spring training.

Yet we never once
went to a game together.
I'm not sure if he ever
made it to Fenway.

Years after his death
my dad told me how
he once went to visit
Grampa at the State Hospital
  there were no rehab clinics
  in the '50s

and he was nearly
hit in the head
by a baseball
thrown by another patient
  inmate(?)
jealous that no one
had come to visit
him.

Our family has
no history,
no stories passed down,
only secrets
that we cling to
ferociously.

What went on
in that house?
When did he leave
my grandmother?
  my father?
    my aunts and uncle?
What circumstances
broke this family?

Was he a violent drunk?
A promiscuous drunk?
A social drunk?
A happy drunk?
Or just a
drunk?

Hole = Mouth

After years of labor
Blood, sweat and tears
I'm no closer
To filling this hole
I inherited from
Dear old Dad

I've thrown millions
Of empty beer cans
Whiskey bottles
And hangovers
Into the bottomless pit
To no avail

I've tossed countless
Bags of marijuana
Folds of coke
And handfuls of pills
Down the garbage chute
And the hole got deeper

I briefly tried
To fill the hole
With sexual conquests
With the same results

Rage couldn't fill it
Hatred couldn't fill it
Nothing seemed to fill it
I need some emotional landfill

Ten years later
The hole is getting deeper
My fall is getting steeper

I'm left with one choice
Turn my back on the hole
And walk away

New Doors

Every day I must open
New doors
Take new paths
To find myself
To hell with the rat race
And inevitable ulcers

As a survivor of pain
Most self-inflicted
I must learn to live again
Without crutches
In their many forms

As a wizard of words
I must stretch my mind
Through analytical
Emotional litmus test
Am I mad
Or just insane

As the pessimist leaves
And a realist arrives
I must make the transition
In my point of view
It's not an on / off
Switch
But a gradual fade

I'm tired of scowling
At the first seeds
Of happiness
Just to avoid
A potential heartbreak
I've been slowly grinding
It to dust anyway

As someone who has never
Smelled the roses
Or the burning of books
I look forward to both
Creeping into my life
As I open new doors

Why

Tried so hard
To tear down the fences
Not sure
If it's worth it
  after all
Breaking my back
To break both of our defenses
Think of us
As two people
  not as dolls

Every time
It's the same charade
We both know
The rules of this
  sport of sorts
Both too stubborn
To let the shooting fade
Sleep brings truce
Another day brings
  a war of words

Why
Do we make each other cry?
Why
Can't the competition die?

I've heard all
Of your accusations
You've heard all
Of my sarcastic
  last words

We both know
This entire conversation
Line by line
We both say things
The other never heard

The thinnest piece of paper
Is being torn in half
Nothing to hold it together
Every bond's been ripped apart

Knife cuts deeper with every thrust
Twisting, slicing inner strength
Blade severs the blind man's trust
Longest rope is at its length

The screams end
Two souls sit in seclusion
The walls keep
Two hearts
  so far apart
Hunting another
Partner in lustful confusion
The walls keep growing
The blade keeps thrusting
  in the dark

Why?

Help

I try to tell myself
It will be different
   next time
But I know it won't

If there even is a next time
I will act just the same
And so will she

I can't help but walk away
You can't help but follow

Remnants of day dreams
Ashes of nightmares
Nothing left to prove I was there

Can't escape our pasts
They twist and turn together
Nothing to show our directions

I can't help but leave
You can't help but stay

The sky's the limit
For me and my future
Yet I anchor myself to an island

Loving and hating is my nature
Neither or both, take it or leave it
Where does that leave us?

I can't help but wonder
You can't help me at all

Just when I thought I'd figure out
Everything about you, me, us, the world
You surprise me again, and I cry

Nothing is certain
Nothing is like it seems
That's for certain
  Confusing?
  You bet!

I can't help you
You can't help me
We can't help ourselves

Midnight Blue

Once again I'm
Drowning in emotions
That I don't
Care to name
Never mind
Experience
Emotions that jangle
Together like a pocket
Full of keys

Four souls
Snatched from my
Immediate circle
Within eight days
By the never ending
Death machine

Four lives
Four deaths
Four gut-wrenching stories
Four volumes of painful memories
One blunt question
That no impassioned preacher
Can gloss over
To my satisfaction
WHY?

I'm feeling blue
Twilight blue
Midnight blue
The deepest, darkest blue
The blue just before
The black

All choked up on nothing
Nothing but pain
Deep down
Midnight blue
Pain
Can't swallow this
Lump of
Pain

I sit here bleeding grief
All over my naked soul
My agony
My loss
My mourning
My midnight blue

– In loving memory of:
Vilem Pospisil, Don Steele, Miriam Iszard & Emil Matero

Anger

Anger grips and shakes me
Thrashes my rock-solid sensibilities
Turns me into an emotional
Irrational, spiteful man

Anger twists my gut
Steps on my heart
Spits on my soul
Leaves me disgusted
With the human race

Anger vaults my heart rate
Strips my insulation of
Calculated cynicism
Shatters my illusion of control

Anger steals what little
Peace I have managed to accumulate
Replacing it with piss and vinegar
Like only anger can do

It takes me hours
To regain my composure
Although I am predictably
Several notches lower
On the self-esteem meter

It takes all my willpower
To withstand the urge to blurt
Out my frustration and pain
To bite my tongue until it bleeds
Rather than expose my emotions

It takes twenty deep breaths
Countless affirmations
A few bear hugs and occasionally
One stiff drink
To relocate my center of gravity

It takes all kinds in this world
My kind, your kind
The kind of jerk who spreads
Anger like a shovel full of manure.

Silent Trees

Today I saw silent
trees being bent
by the wind,
neither complaining
nor breaking,
withstanding
the elements
outside their control,
simply waiting for
calm.

Trees know
they can not stop
the wind,
to even try
would be a waste
of time and energy.

They allow themselves
to be swayed,
confident
in their roots'
ability
to grasp what really matters,
confident that
no matter how strong the wind,
no matter how far they must
bend in response,
no matter how hard it rains,
or how long the winter,
trees will be there
when the calm is restored.

Dig in with your roots.
Hold on to your family
  tree.
Weather the storms
knowing the wind
can not move you,
the rain can not
wash you away,
tomorrow brings
another day,
  another season,
    another year.

Trees don't try
to control their
surroundings,
they react out of
faith in their survival.

Sometimes I Speak

Arguing with gravity
Death and
Pain

Scolding human nature
Vengeance
Lust

Righting wrongs
Larger than mountains
Older than sin

Protesting time's ticking
Nightfall's darkness
Winter's frozen, frigid
Cold

Spreading rumors about
Oncoming trains
And tornadoes

Screaming at the glaciers
To hurry
The hell up

Ranting at autumn's foliage
Frost

Venting about the merciless
Sun

Lecturing Mother Nature
About what's fair
And what's not

Whining at her droughts
Nagging at her floods
Bitching at her earthquakes
  her volcanoes
    her Ice Age coming
To set us all straight

Begging
The canyons to close
The rain to cease
The clouds to turn
Red, purple, green

Sometimes I speak
Simply to fill
The awkward silence

Trying to coax
A smile
From my vacant soul

Your Empty Spaces

I will be the yin
to your yang,
melting,
reshaping
my soul, to fit
inside your
empty spaces,
inside your shadows.

Tired

Tired
of it all,
of the stress,
of the frustration.
Just plain old
tired.

Sick and tired
of the futility,
of the accusations,
of the paranoia.
Sick and tired
of the redundancy.

I'm tired
physically,
mentally,
emotionally.
Completely
exhausted.

Tired
of the sixty-hour work weeks,
with no money after the bills.
Tired
of the second guessing,
both by and of me.
Tired
of waiting for my day,
my turn, my victory.

Most of all
I'm tired
of being
tired.

Birth

Egg shell
Cracking
Two halves
Splitting
Poor, unsuspecting
Soul
Dropped into the
Frying pan

Didn't Mean To…

Didn't mean to drag your tears
Out like a magnet
Didn't mean to bruise
Your fragile soul

Sometimes we can read
Each other's mind
But some days
Like today
The reception is poor
Mistakes and misunderstandings
Turn into missiles of pain
We never meant to launch

Both of us are improving
In so many ways
Separately and together
I sometimes forget
It's two steps forward
And one step back
But it's still one step
In the right direction

Didn't mean to drag you down
Like a whirlpool
Didn't mean to drown
My giggling girl

5.

Count Basie Saved My Soul

Pain, Like Energy

I find it difficult to choose
words or form sentences
that express my confusion,
my conviction,
my constant state of discontent,
so I do the best I can
through fragmented verse,
painting around the picture
hoping my heart will show itself
not due to an unwillingness
to speak the truth
but out of my inability
to identify it.

Discussion seems to create conflict,
and conflict brings pain,
so I avoid it at all costs,
yet I can not extinguish
the core feelings
which accumulate until they burst
out my eyes, mouth and soul.

Pain, like energy
can never be dissipated
only transferred from one source,
one generation, one conversation,
to another.

Past wounds long discarded
to the scrap heap of outdated feelings
creep back into our shadow dance
making it nearly impossible
to separate the overlapping layers
of anger, grief and shame,

the past, the present and my fears
of the future.

A single disagreement
thrown on the pile
becomes a mountain
of irreconcilable differences.

So I ask you,
a woman stronger than gravity,
yet more fragile than silence,
please don't get so close
that I can't breathe or run away
and in return I will try to remember
laughter isn't necessarily an insult
and trust isn't always
a bottomless pit of disappointment.

Distance and Distract

I'm down right now.
I'm depressed
about my stagnant "career"
wallowing in my self-pity,
my helplessness,
my best friend.

I don't feel like writing
an insightful, clever poem
to burn off some creative steam.
I don't feel like attacking
this problem or being cheered up.

I just want to sit here
and be blue.
Actually that's not correct.
I really don't know
what I want to do.

I only know
what I don't want.
I don't want this,
I don't want that.
I don't want to talk
to anyone about anything.
I don't want to confront
my antagonists.
I don't want to do anything.

I want to distance and distract
myself from this discouragement,
this disappointment.
I want to eat or drink anything
I can get my hands on.

I want to stuff these feelings
so far down my gut
they will take weeks to resurface.

I want to sleep, the only way
to totally shut out the pain,
at least until I wake or
it follows me through nightmares.

I want to intoxicate myself
by any means available
to stop this negativity
throbbing in my skull.

I want to listen to music,
read a book, jump off a bridge,
do anything but sit here and
think about this for one more second.

So what do I do?
I overanalyze it
like everything else in my life.

The Sound

The sound
of rain
falling,

not the
splatter
upon impact,

but the roar
of a pissed off
Mother Nature

dumping gallons
of water through
the hollow sky,

the drone of a
waterfall
without end,

or a river
flowing
through mid air,

the sound
of water crashing
against itself,

the sound
of blood
being spilled,

the sound
of promises
being broken,

the sound
that woke me,
humbled me,

bruised me
deeper than I
was prepared for.

Count Basie Saved My Soul

On this torrential Tuesday
wrapped in a musty
gray blanket of
flash flood warnings,
I find it extremely
vital to declare
that Count Basie
saved my soul.

If it wasn't for
"Kansas City Wrinkles,"
I might never have learned
to truly relax,
a lifetime riddled
with futile attempts
to locate the serenity
that was waiting
for me all along
within jazz music.

If I hadn't discovered
the Count bouncing
across the airwaves,
if he hadn't rescued
my long forgotten,
abused and atrophied
love of music,
I might still be
hating life and myself.

That one tune
taught me to rejoice,
to release,
to live once again,
albeit at a different pace.

I learned to slow down
my hectic thought patterns
for a few moments,
be still
and relish the purity
of a horn solo,
twelve notes,
music from the soul.

If it wasn't for
Count Basie
and "Kansas City Wrinkles"
I might never have
connected with Coltrane,
Miles, Monk, or any
of the soothing grooves
that I lean on
when this old world
crashes down on me.

I Really Lost It

I lost my temper
Last night
Or should I say
My temper found me

I felt like a jet
Screaming through
Empty ice blue sky
Leaving a thin trail
Of white thread
To show where my rage
Had been

Today that precise trail
Of smoking anger
Has faded and blurred
To a puffy, smudged
Cloud of gray regret

Did I really need to
Win?
My tongue says "no"
But my heart knows the sad
Truth

Lately I feel like a rock
Buried in a river bed
Swallowed and smothered
In a liquid prison
Out of my control

Life is washing by me
  over me
    through me
Out of my control

I can't seem to get
Along with my wife
My son or myself
And the more I'm around
The worse it gets

Will it ever get any
Better?
My mind says "yes"
But my broken heart
Fears the sad, pathetic
Truth

The trouble with running
From your problems
Is that you bring
Yourself with you

If Only

Driving along a darkened
Coastal highway
As the black ocean
Licks gray sand
With ivory moonlit waves

Why can't my life
Be that simple?

If only I could
Stop measuring time
With such calculated greed

If only I could
Stop collecting scars
With perverted pleasure

If only I could
Relax like raindrops
Falling, yet ignoring the ground

If only I could
Remind myself that
A smile is not a weapon

If only I could
Make up my mind
About anything, free of doubt

If only I could
Put into words
That which burns my soul

If only I could
End this bitter
Refusal to ever simply agree

If only I could
Let go of my need
To be right, to be strong

If only I could
Wash away years of
Spontaneous combustion

If only I could
Snap my fingers
And make it all go away

If only

There is Nothing

There is nothing
like hardship
to force you to embrace
what is integral in your life,
nothing like poverty
to show you how valuable
your loved ones are,
nothing like pain
to illuminate joy.

After days, months, years
of struggle
through depression,
in the midst of endurance,
waist deep in consolation,
yearning for luxury,
waiting for serenity,
I have once again
had the wind knocked
out of my soul,
I have seen over the next hill
and was petrified
by what my eyes witnessed:

another thousand
dollars in auto repairs,
a job on the verge of
disintegrating into hunger,
a career still miles
from developing,
a three-year-old son
with no food, no clothes,
  no dad if I succumb
  to my suicidal urges.

When I ponder this near
future, a decision must be made.
Do I step further into
this quicksand of doubt,
willingly drown in my self-pity
or do I focus on the marvel
of a growing child,
Southern California weather,
creative work in the field of my choice,
support of those I surround myself with?

As much as it goes
against my nature
I must take the second path.

A Barefoot Boy

When this prison sentence
some call life
starts squeezing down on me,
I close my eyes
and picture my childhood
in New England;
a time and place
that no longer exist,
even if I wanted to return.

I picture the lush green forests,
multicolored leaves of autumn,
orange, red, golden leaves,
purple lilacs,
pink skies before sunset,
gray face of Cathedral Ledge,
white snow and brown mud,

the leisurely pace
of rural America
(circa 1975),
I remember the calm
of childhood, the peace
of small town roads,
the songs of crickets,
frogs and my personal
favorite, the whip-o-wil,

I remember rivers with fish
  (and water)
Little League ball fields
with whole neighborhoods
in attendance,
a four-room school house,

dogs howling at the 12
o'clock fire whistle,

a barefoot boy
riding his bike
until dusk,
I trace his steps,
breathe his air,
hear his heartbeat.

I realize
I wouldn't go back
even if it were possible,
I have too much invested in the present,
but it certainly
serves its purpose:
momentary tranquility,
time away from the storm.

33

Today I'm still pessimistic,
resistant to the slightest
change,
incapable of the most
basic social exchange.

Yet, today I'm happier
than years past,
more content than I can recall
for quite some time,
certainly more comfortable
than I've ever been before.

I laugh a bit more,
mostly thanks to my three
year old son.
Don't tell anyone, but
I even sing and dance
with him in the privacy
of our three-bedroom apartment.

I have discovered a handful
of soothing tools
to lubricate my existence
against the friction of
this cold, harsh world.
Thank God for jazz music,
reading, writing and the
Stanley Cup playoffs.

Looking at a freshly
cleansed Santa Monica sky,
I realize I no longer
hate life,

just people.
No, that's not true.
It's only the assholes
in traffic,
on the phone,
in my face,
with their mouths open
and their eyes closed,
spewing their ignorance
while ignoring the truth.

All I want
for my birthday
is 24 hours
where no one disagrees
with me,
I won't be greedy,
start making ridiculous demands,
just one day
of the world
marching to my drum beat.

You might actually see
me smile.

Aries

1,800
miles per hour
That's how fast
our planet
screams through darkness
while the earth
I stand on
appears to remain
in place.

That's how I experience
this stretch of cruel
and unusual existence:

While you all inhabit
a steady world
of black, white, true
and false,
simple decisions,

I am overanalyzing
my very own breath,
how to maximize the
oxygen intake to
expended energy ratio.

I am searching
for the hidden
superior angle,
the truth inside
the riddle.

A walk in the park
or a trip to the market

becomes a roller
coaster ride
through a sea
of poisonous
smiles.

Certain Things

When I least expect it, peace creeps up behind me.
I listen to soulful tunes, catch the mildest buzz,
wash dishes and write a poem.

No voices clutching at my attention
No unspoken contracts of servitude
No borders, no boundaries.

Certain things can still bring a smile to my stern jaw,
start my head nodding in a loose rhythm
Fill my lungs with air

Certain things I have forgotten
or left behind with my youth

Sudden death overtime hockey
Seventh game of the Stanley Cup finals

Anytime an underdog perseveres

Music that shakes your entire body

A child's laughter

What else is there?

For Once

For once
the angry man
is not me.
I'm not even his accomplice.

For once
I'm the one watching from a distance
as another man rages
at everything that goes against
his perfect plan.

For once
I am refusing
to be tangled up
in another's web.
So glad I am not him.

For once
I am smiling in the heat
of battle,
at peace with myself
at least for today.

What Have You Forgotten?

people learn to hate
people learn to wait
sooner or later
we all accept our fate

    I yam
    what I yam
    and that's all
    that I yam

I've been running
on broken toes
blistered ankles
and not enough sleep

    never enough
    of anything
    never enough

once I was amazed
that we actually made it
to the illustrious 1984
then 1999, 2000, 2001…

I'm 36 with nothing left
to look forward to
but my son's
various milestones

    the first this
    the first that
    the latest
    the greatest
    the essence of all
    I've lost

first grade
my god
my son
is in the first grade

I can already see
the chinks in his armor
his Achilles' heels
proof of his parents' imperfections
but on a good day
I see how much he sparkles
and must admit
he's the product of our strengths

At which point
did I lose sight of my path
and wander into this
miserable repetition

or is this still
the path I've chosen
the scenic route
to hell

lost my rough edges
I've sacrificed me
forgotten how to relax
don't remember how to

    feel
    think
    listen
    write
    love
    smile

what have you forgotten

   in your haste
   in your waste
   in your endless
   cut and paste

rhyming schemes
lining screams
with a series of
broken dreams

on and on I go!

I Remember

Lately I've been spending more time reminiscing. These are usually stolen in 30-second intervals throughout the day, swimming in a score of repeating memories.

I remember playing alone, always playing something alone.

I played sports mostly, since sports were my life from the age of 8-16. And I played them alone. Baseball was easy. Toss the ball a foot into the air, wait for it to drop, then swing the bat. Or throw a tennis ball against the wall, field the rebound, then repeat the process until sun down.

I would reenact entire ball games, taking swings for each batter, controlling each inning, to create a 9th inning hero. I would envision runner's progress, pitching changes, every detail. Alone.

I would also play entire football games in the same manner. I would throw a ball towards the clouds (kick off), then run it back a few dozen yards before spinning and falling (tackled by the defense). I would reenact play after play. Alone.

Basketball championships were decided either with a dusty ball slipping through a hoop nailed to a tree, or Nerf ball slam dunk.

Hockey was a series of mad dashes, stick handling and last second glory.

And don't even mention wrestling.

It seems my team always won in these testosterone fairy tales. I always got the hit when I needed to. There is a calm that comes with making up the rules as you go (especially with no one watching to complain).

I never consciously thought about it, but I really expected my entire life would be that easy. Just will it to be, and call a foul if you miss the shot.

Here I sit, 35 years old, 60 hours a week erased by "work," few dreams left to ponder.

Alone.

Je vous aime

Quiet rainy days
one of life's treasures
that has slipped from my possession
my consciousness
my reality

We used to hold hands,
laugh for no reason
other than how drenched we had become

Today, my fear is that I'll never
return to that level of peace

How long will I be able to hug my son
before he becomes his own man

I love many things in this world
however I can rarely remember
most of them

All of my spare time
my spare love
my spare strength
my spare anything
goes towards "The Family"

Sometimes it takes a rainy day to remind me
of the other souls who live under this roof
the amazing depth of love waiting for me
the ocean of joy you both swim in
the potential of us all.

Je vous aime
my sweet, sweet family
and one of these days
I'll be home for dinner

My Overwhelmed Soul

Months have snuck past
my over analyzing gaze
without being observed,
appreciated
or documented

My only saving grace
has been my "artistic" renderings

Where is my imagination?

When I need it the most?

This is merely an exercise
a desperate attempt
to relocate my solace

I am about to return
to the state
which I fled from so long ago
(forgive my sappiness, I am so out of practice)

My empty-handed prayer
is that New Hampshire
my brother's wedding
a night with Dad
will somehow restore clarity
in my overwhelmed soul

Swim

To fight
or not to fight

Daily double jeopardy
game show repeat
in syndication

I stand perfectly still
hold my breath and pray
the predator passes me by

I step out of line
my usual grumbles and whispers
manifest through an acid tongue

Recognize a pattern
dance around the truth
one stop ahead of confrontation

I see nothing
I hear nothing
I know nothing

Look back with a smile and sneer
now I slip under the radar
and pick my spots

Please exit
twisting and shouting
as I sing a death march

Any line drawn in the sand
must be crossed in a covert manner
private vindication

wanna join me?
it's a blast!

My demons
  your passion
my fears
  your power
my buttons
  your buttons

Lost and found
I wish I'd drowned
the day you dipped me in the lake

The same lake
I learned to swim, you claim
my sins are washed away

Kids took swimming lessons
in my filth

I'm here
on certain levels
but not yours

I'm strong
in a number of ways
but I have more
than my share of weaknesses

I've awakened
a carnal being
previously encased
with an inferiority complex
instant gratification
at the wrong place and time

I love you
sweat counts for something
and you can count on me

That was then
this is now
when it benefits me

Swim
sinking is not an option
so swim

You don't have to be an Olympian
to tread water
survive the cards you're dealt

Yesterday

Yesterday was dark,
cold and lonely;
nearly the shortest day of the year

The spectacular sunset
was its only redeeming
moment.

A kiss from my son
was the only thing strong enough
to evaporate my tears

Yesterday broke my soul open
My body trembled, wept,
wished to be dead

My Earliest Memory

I am in the car
a station wagon
it is pouring rain
in North Conway
New Hampshire
I am less than five
since my brother
has not yet been born

my mother is crying
she is driving through
tears and windshield wipers

she is crying
over my dad
I don't know why
but I know it is him

come to think of it
I don't recall seeing
my dad until at least six
living in Redstone
in a closet called
a mobile home

back to my mom
weeping behind the wheel
pouting I'm sure

dad is out
with the boys
fixing a stock car
drinking beer
looking at a smiling girl

covered in bubbles
on an auto parts calendar
forearms covered in grease
knuckles bleeding

we are crying
in a thunderstorm
we are crying
where are you

dad built a race car
for me one Christmas
according to the color photo
i couldn't say for sure

the next thing I know
I'm an angry young man

Printed in the United States
98543LV00003BB/240/A